# The Slightly Silly Pocket & Purse

# ANIMAL ALPHABET

## Coloring Book

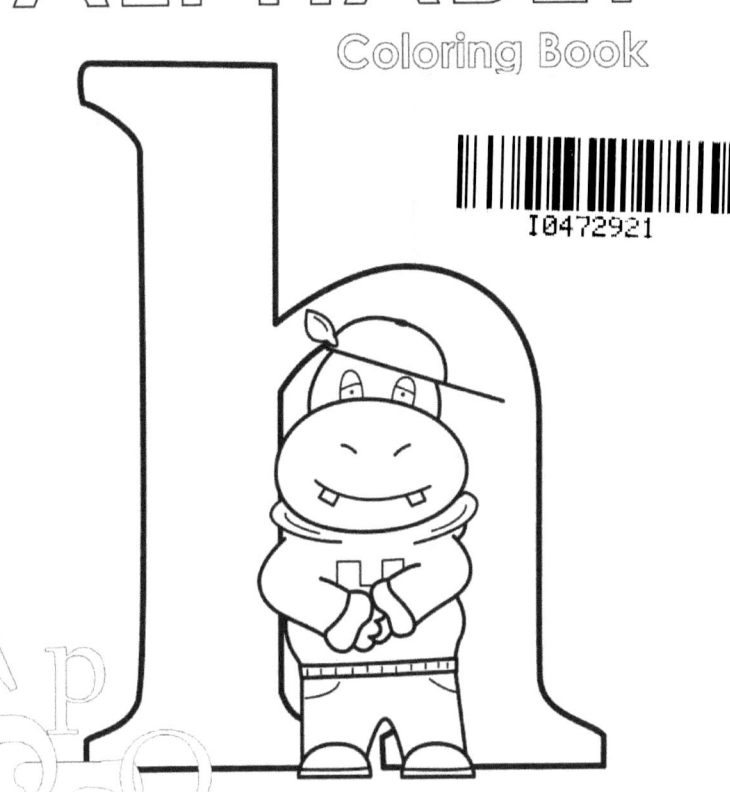

By Valerie Coulman

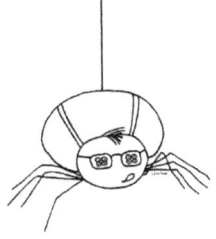

This book began as a weekly challenge on Twitter and I am grateful for that generous community and the fun that exists there. To see how these and other animals of the alphabet were drawn & colored, follow @AnimalAlphabets.

My thanks to Ben Durham (@Calvitre_) for his help in converting my pencil doodles to digital line drawings.

To find more
coloring pages and resources,
visit
www.valeriecoulman.com

A is for ------ ------

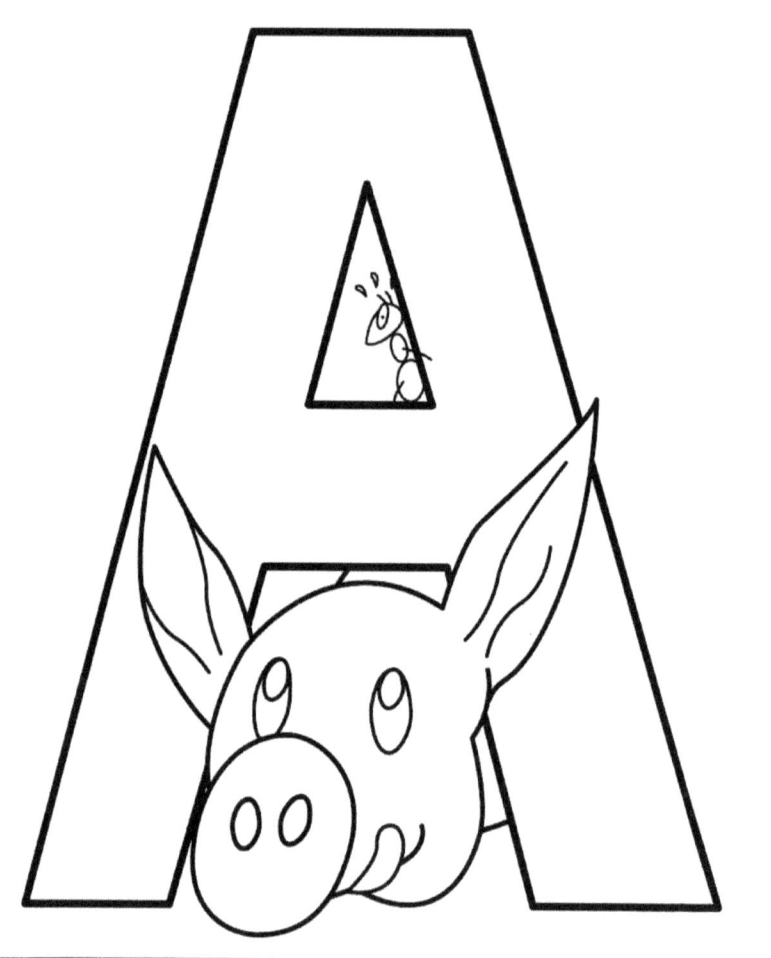

------ ------ Aardvark

B is for

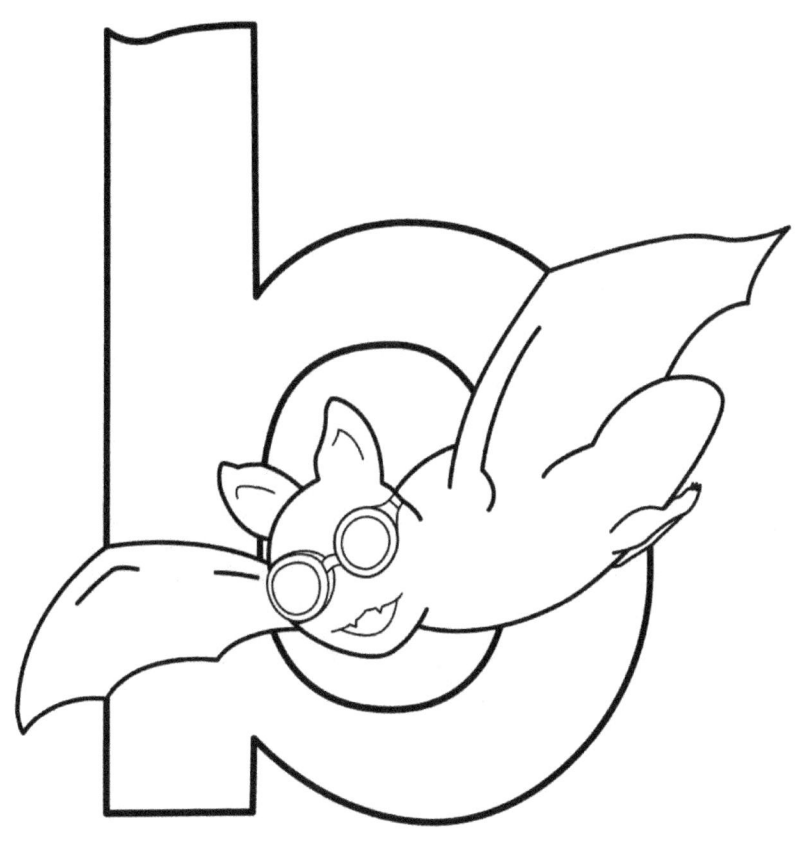

Bat

C is for _____

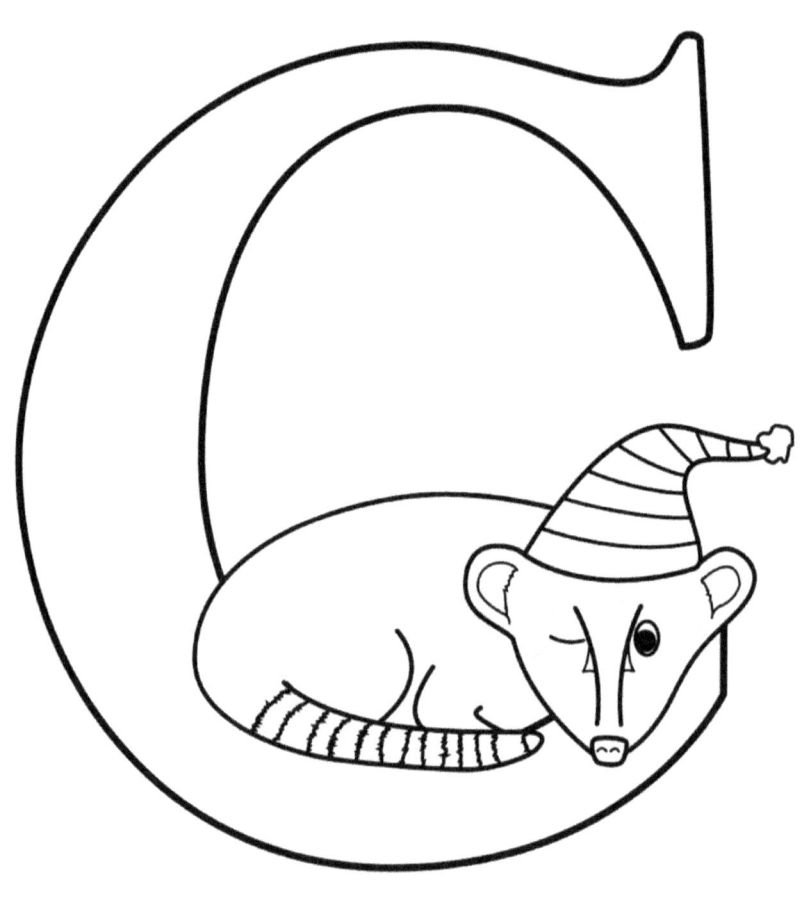

_ _ _ _ _ _ _ _ _ _ _ Coati

D is for _ _ _ _ _ _ _ _ _ _ _ _ _ _

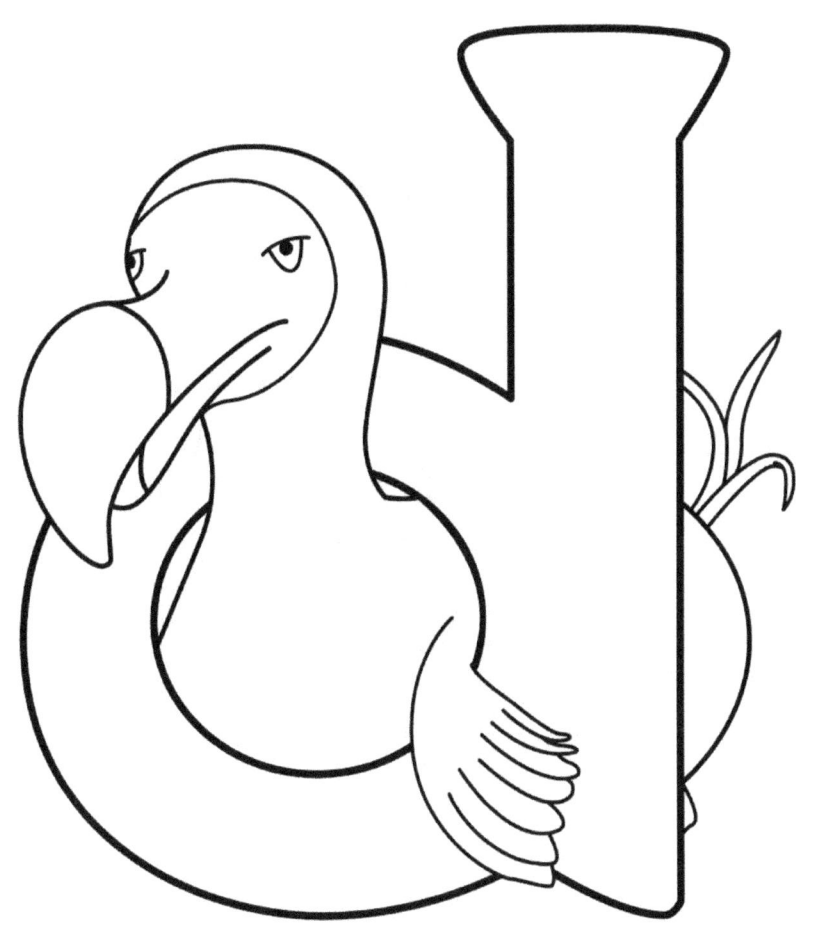

_ _ _ _ _ _ _ _ _ _ _ _ Dodo

# E is for

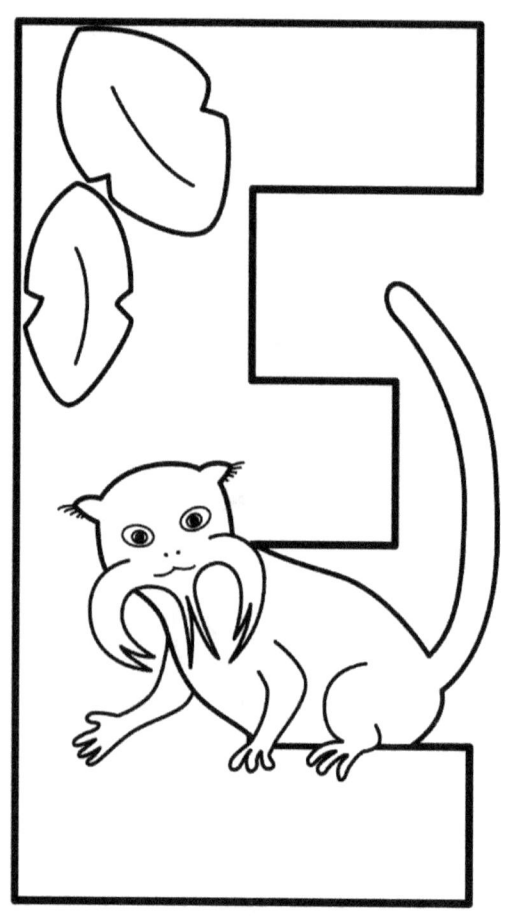

# Emperor Tamarin

F is for _____

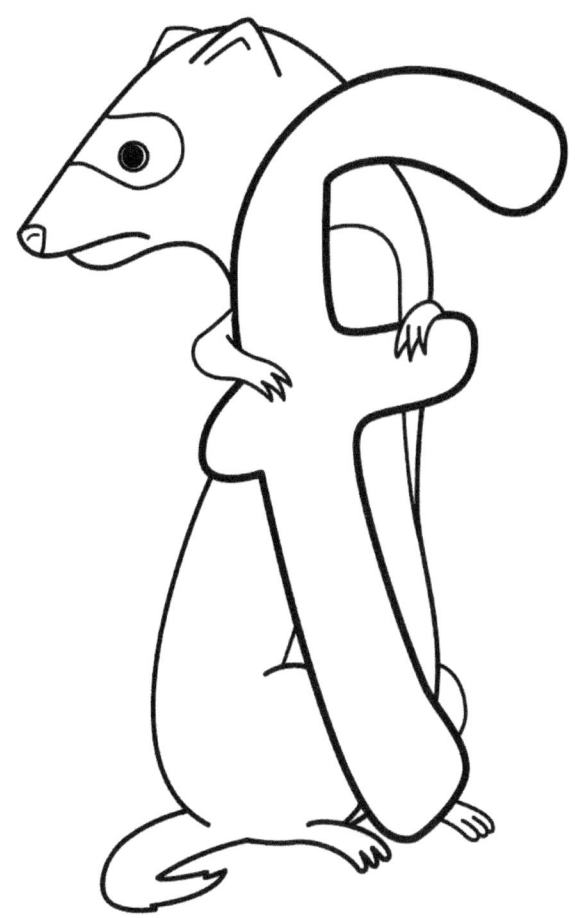

_____ Ferret

G is for

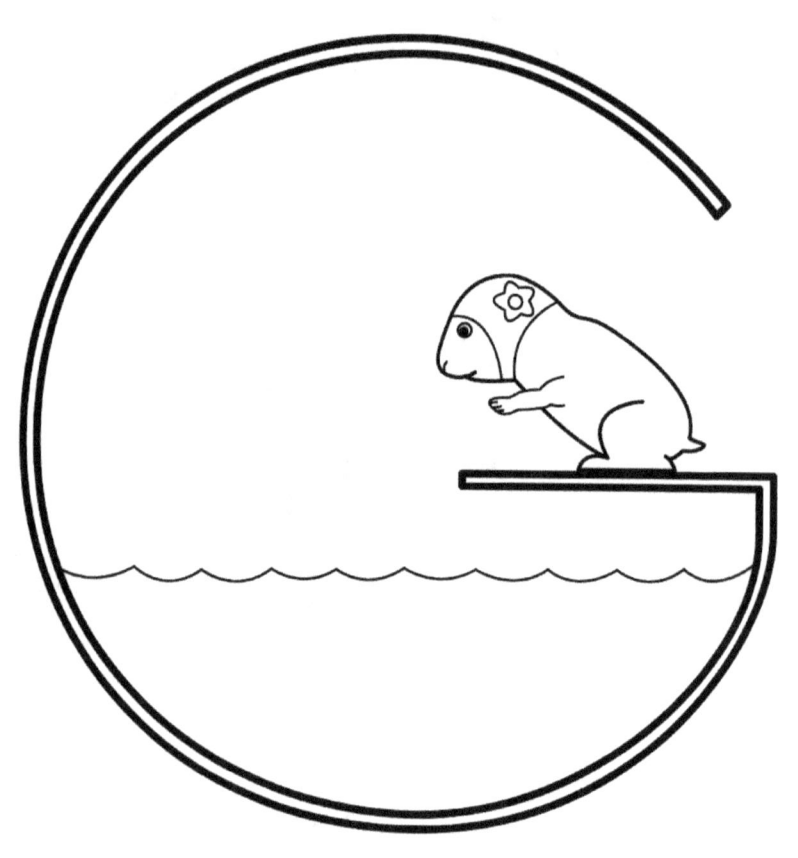

Guinea Pig

H is for ------------------

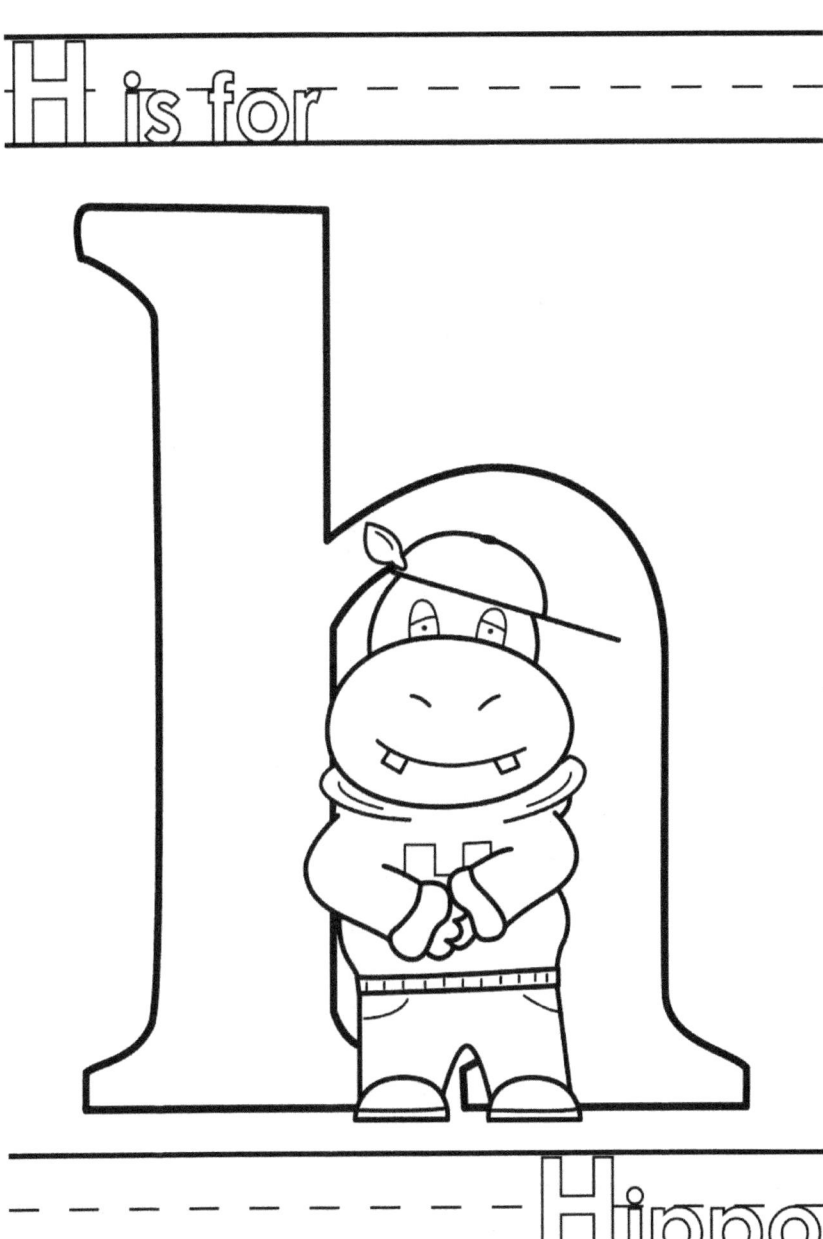

------------ Hippo

I is for _____ Ibex

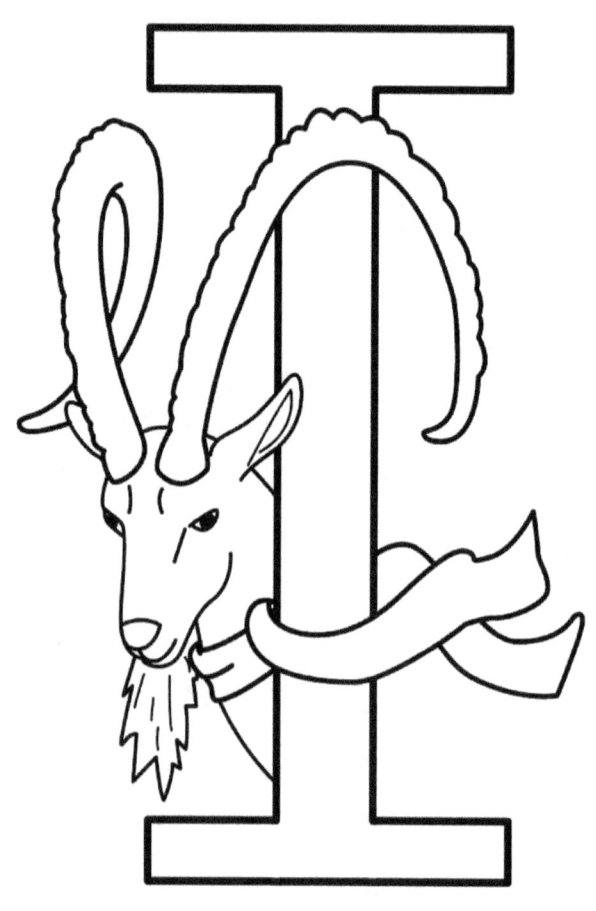

_____ Ibex

# J is for Japanese

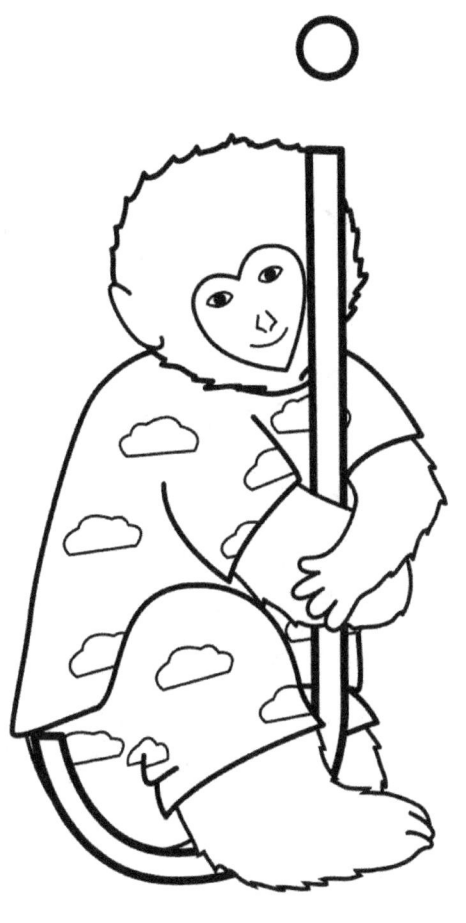

# Macaque

K is for

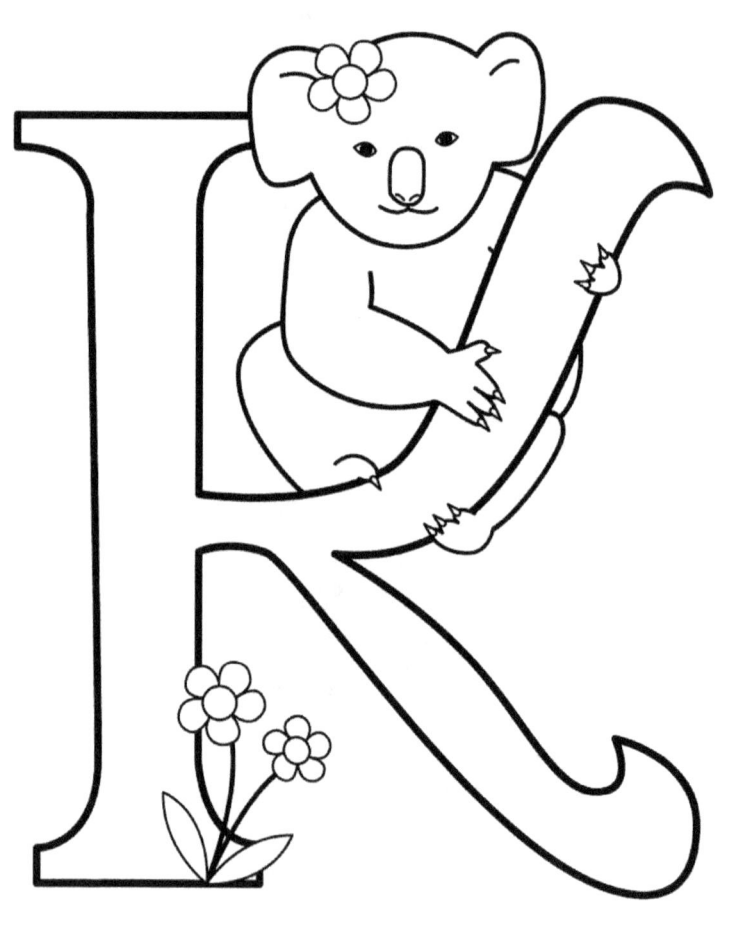

Koala

L is for

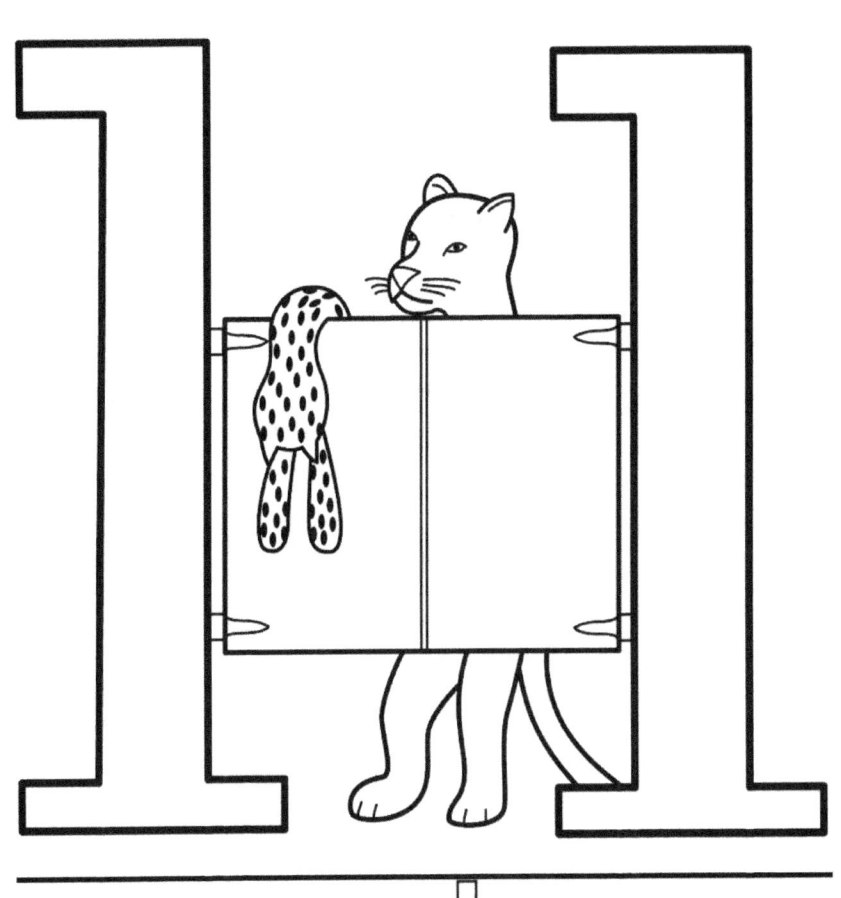

Leopard

M is for ------

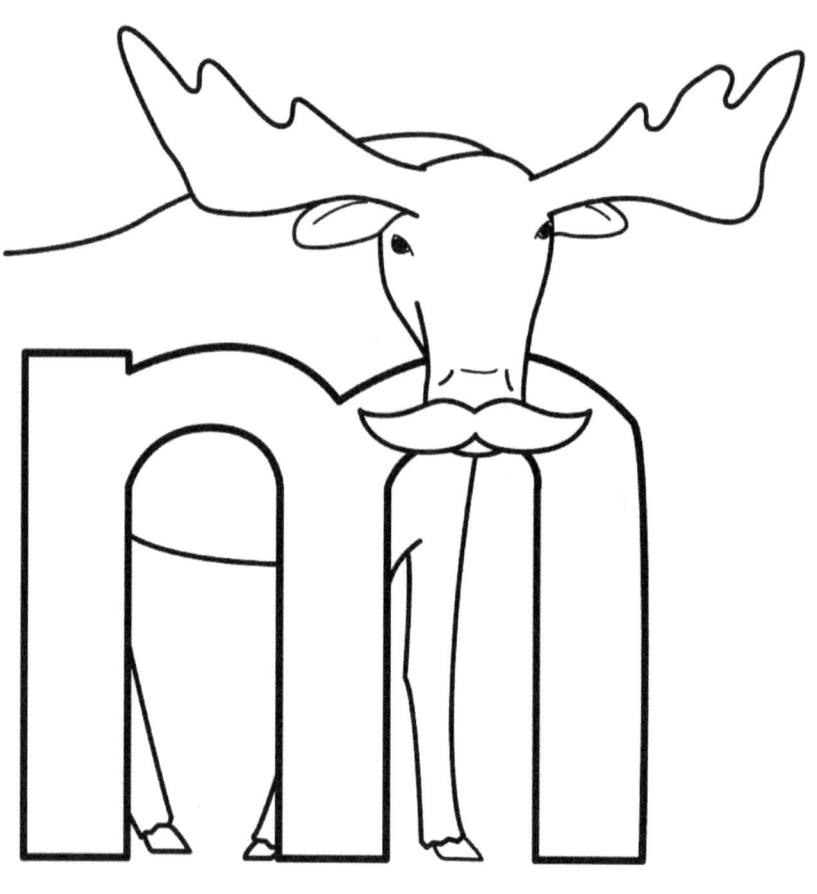

Moose

N is for

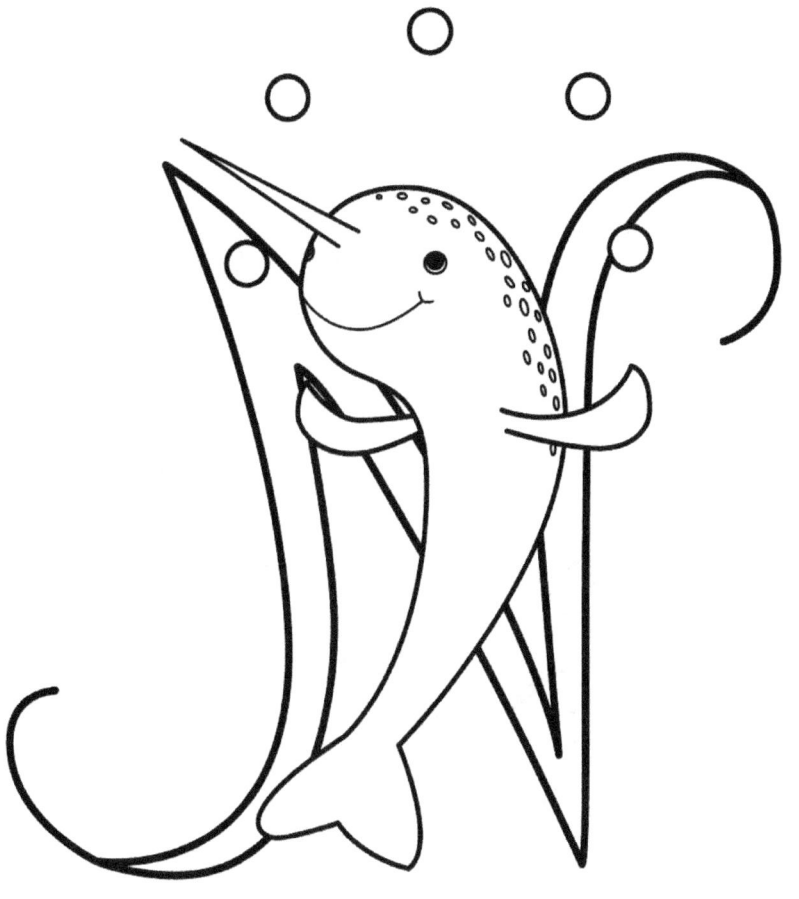

Narwhal

O is for _ _ _ _ _ _ _ _

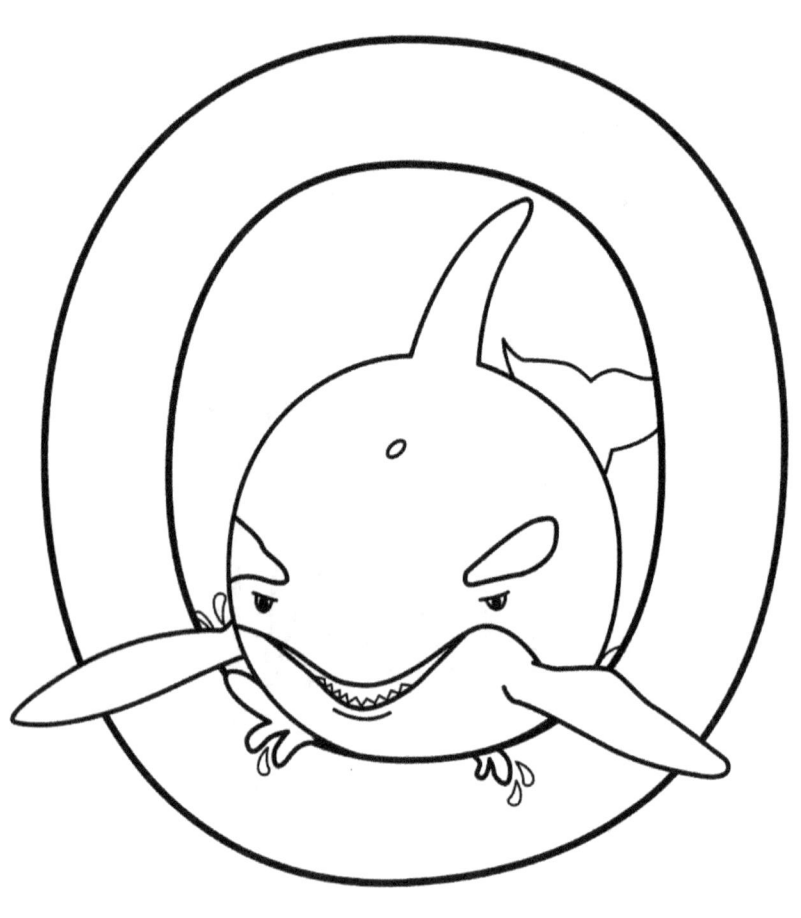

_ _ _ _ _ _ _ _ _ _ Orca

P is for

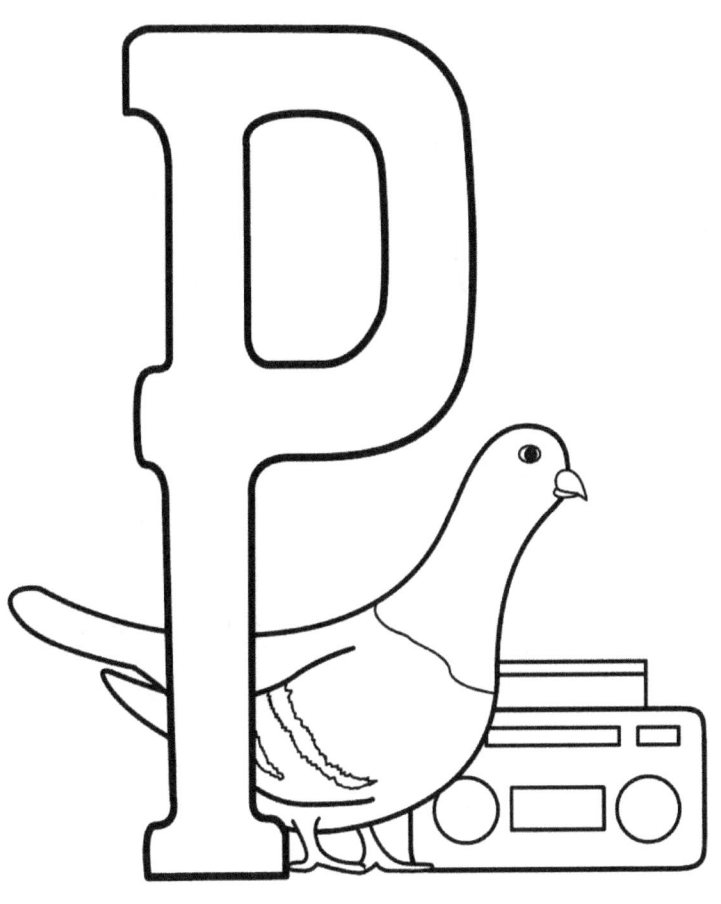

Pigeon

Q is for

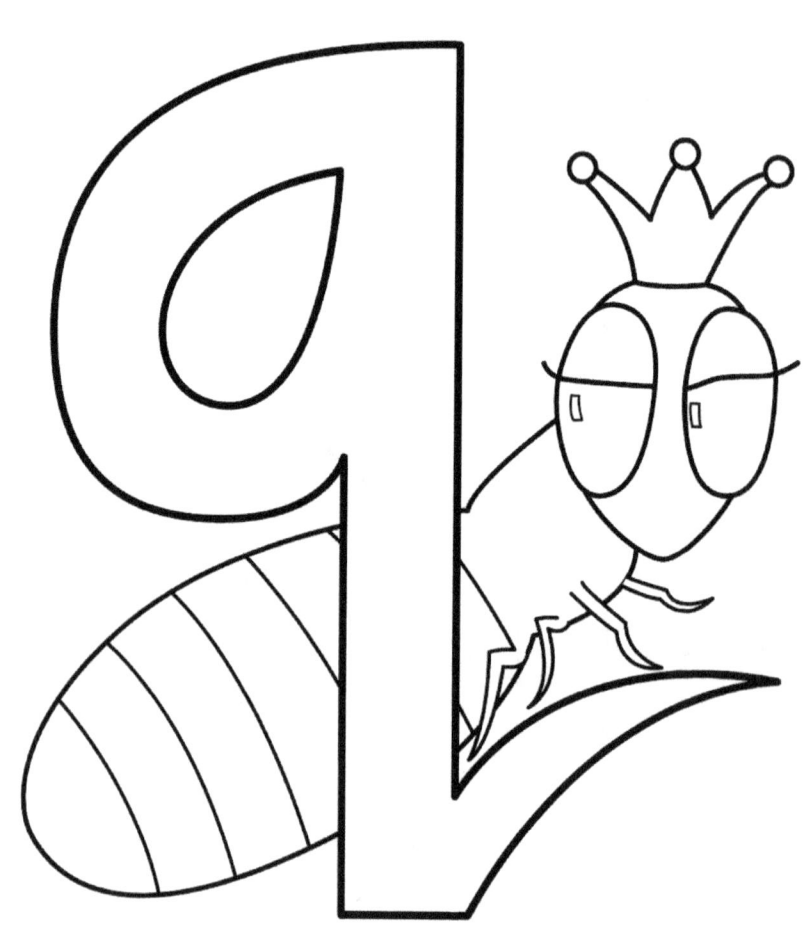

Queen Bee

R is for

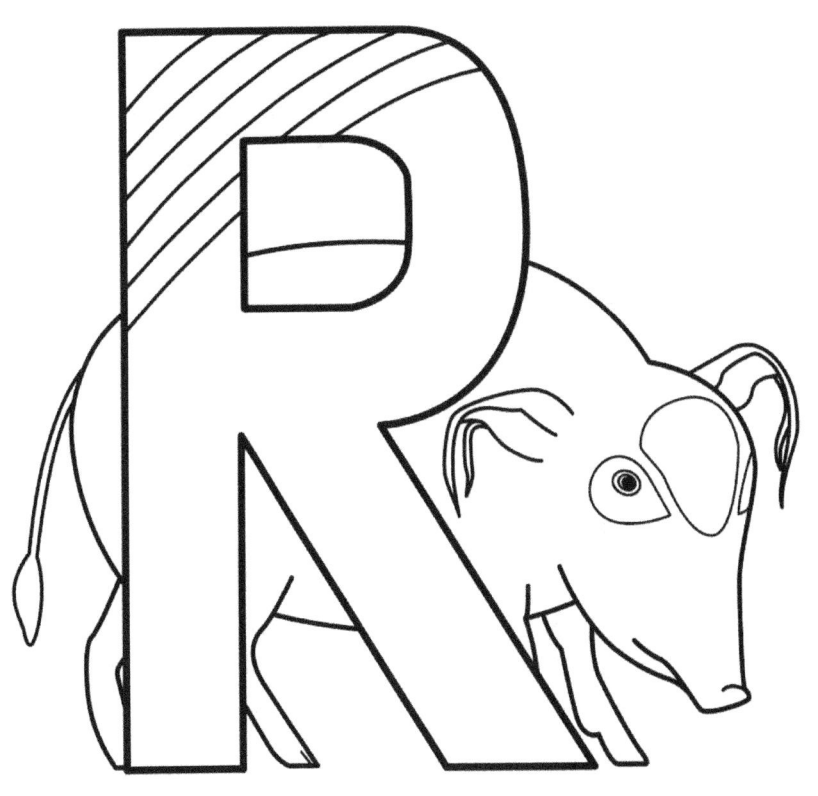

Red River Hog

S is for

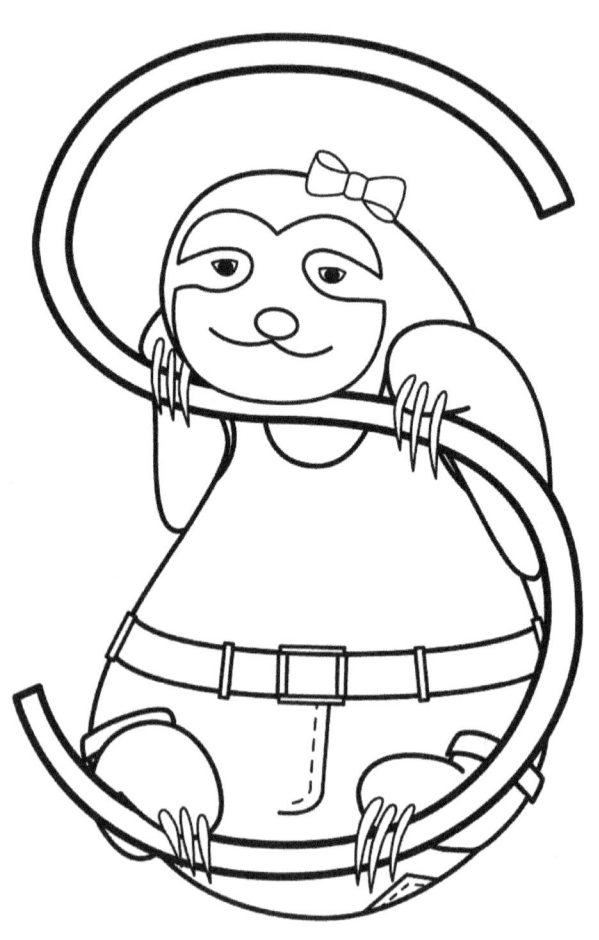

Sloth

T is for

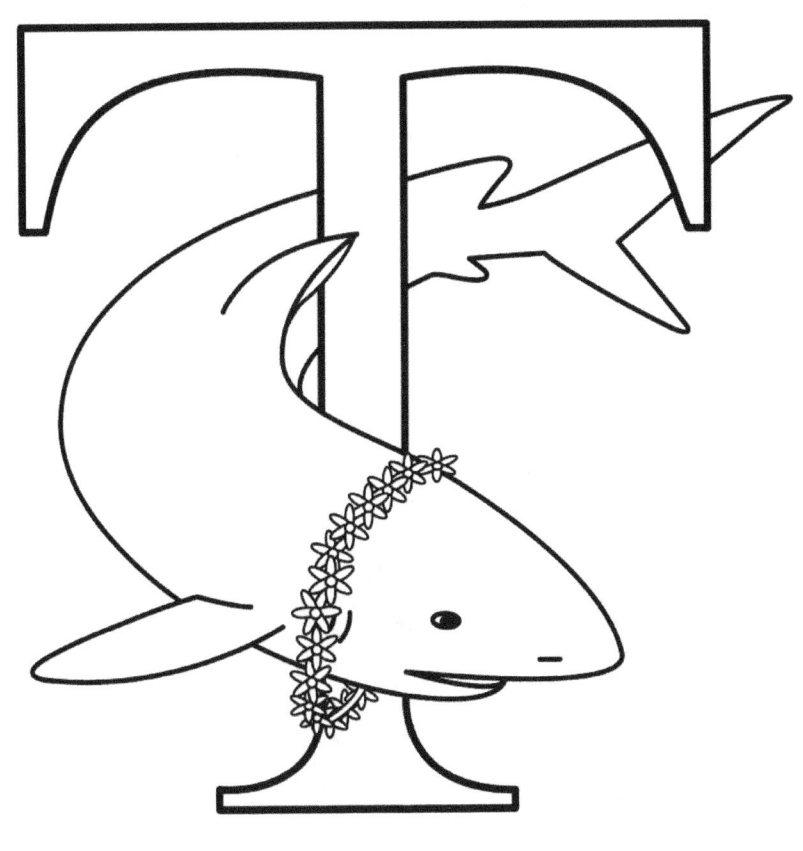

Tiger Shark

U is for

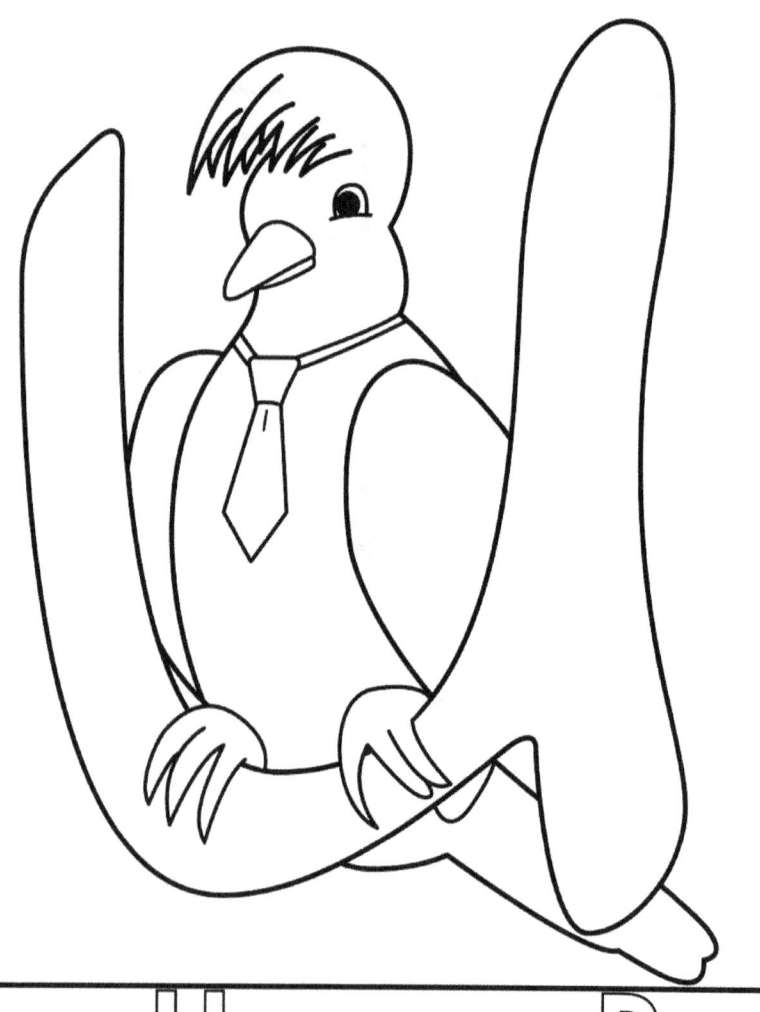

Umbrella Bird

V is for

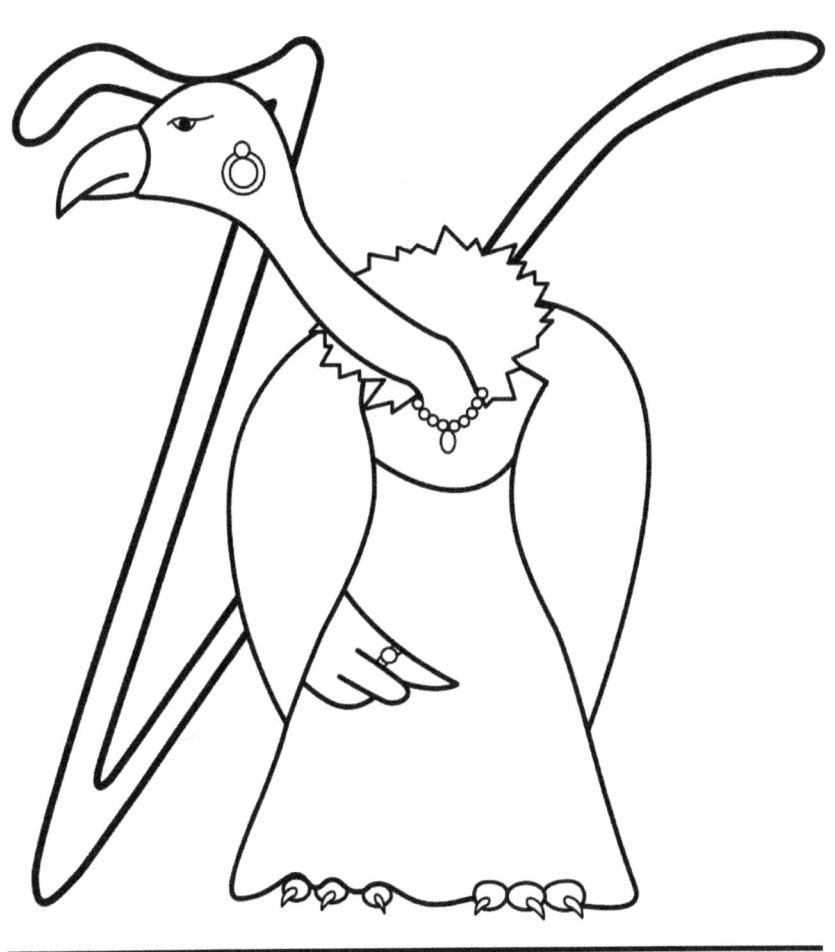

Vulture

# W is for _____

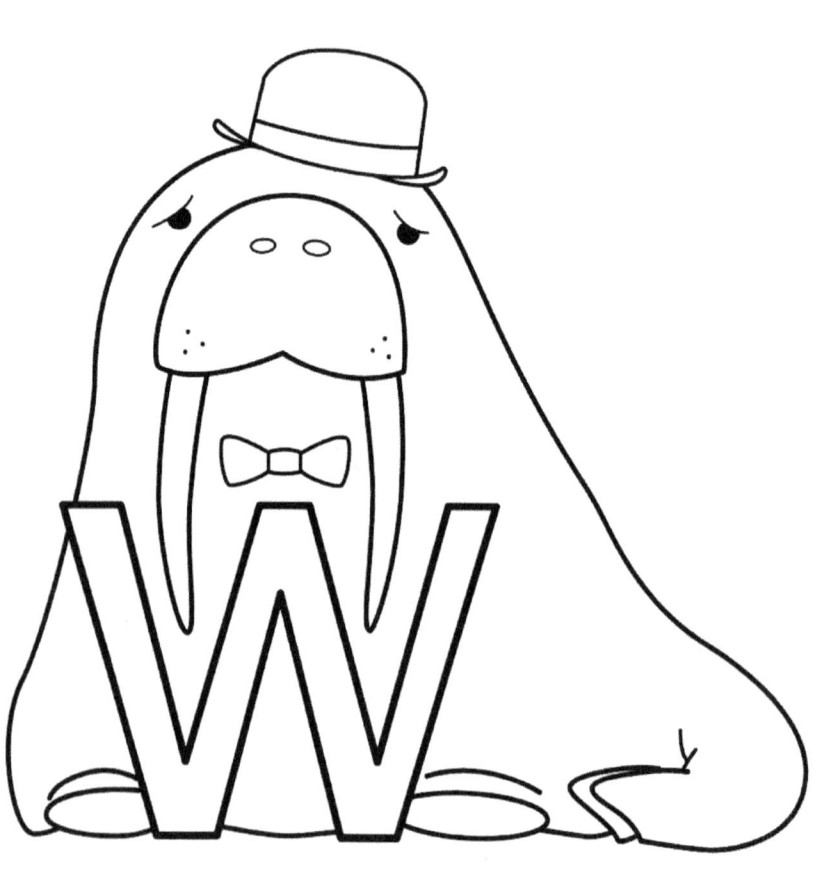

_____ Walrus

# X is for

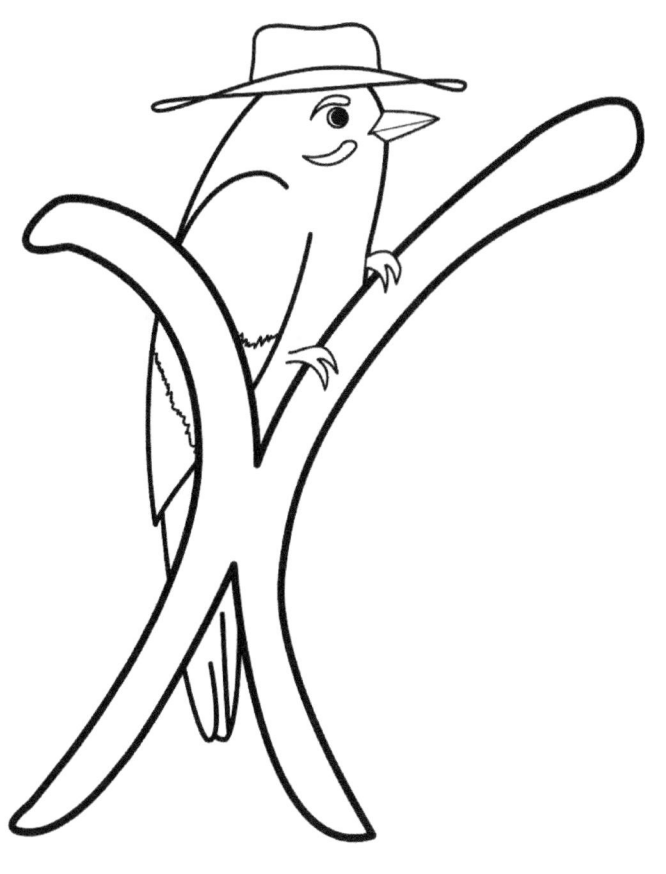

# Xenops

Y is for _ _ _ _ _ _ _ _ _ _ _ _

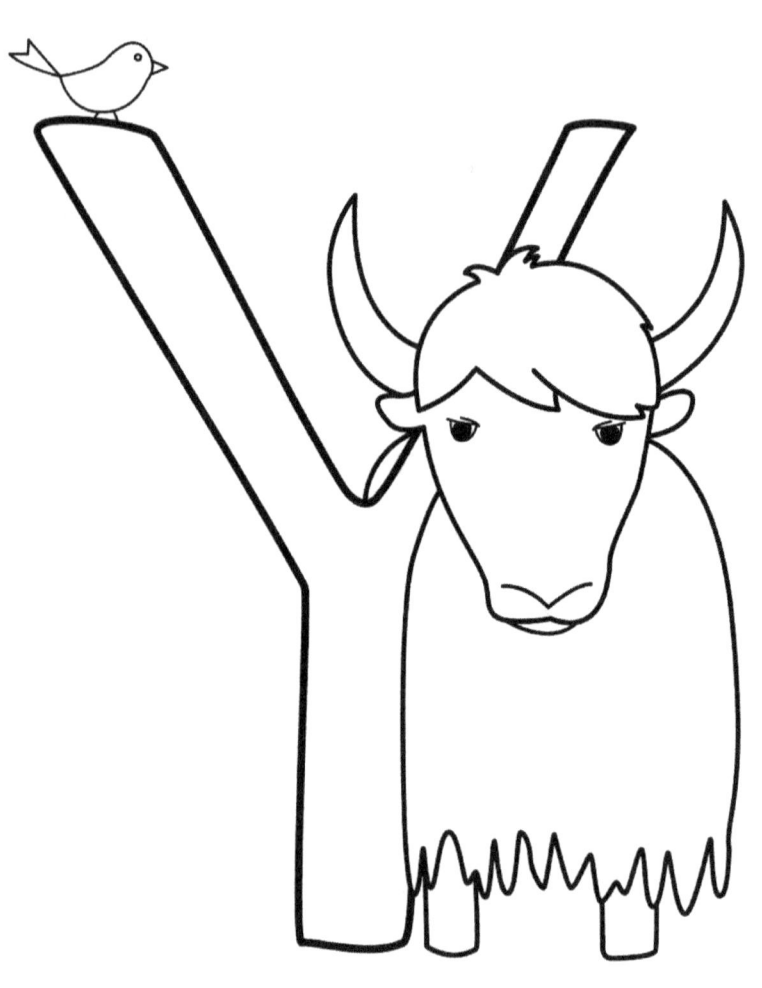

_ _ _ _ _ _ _ _ _ _ _ _ _ _ _ Yak

Z is for

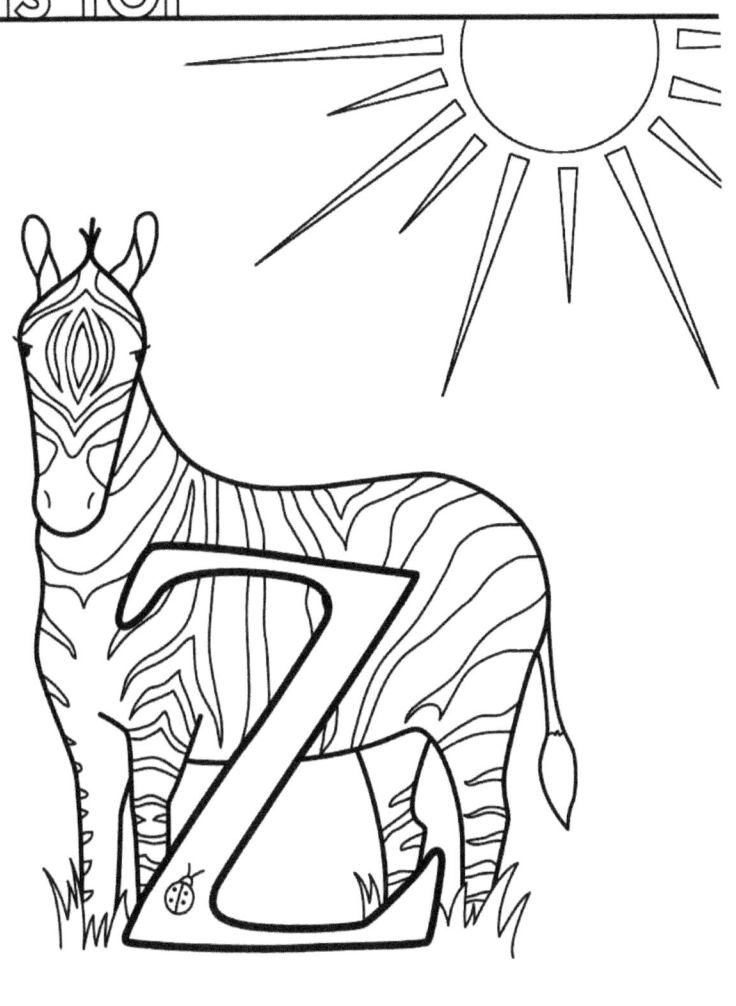

Zebra

# Now it's your turn !

(What do you like to draw?)